T0394872

LIBRARY OF
AWESOME ANIMALS

GLASS FROG

By Janie Scheffer

BEARPORT
PUBLISHING

Minneapolis, Minnesota

Credits

Cover and title page, © Cover and title page, © Daniel Nunez/Nature Picture Library; 3, © creativenature.nl/Adobe Stock; 4–5, © David/Adobe Stock; 7, © LeePhotos/Adobe Stock; 9, © Milan Zygmunt/Shutterstock; 10–11, © Rob Jansen/Shutterstock; 13, © Frank Deschandol & Philippe Sabine/Biosphoto; 14–15, © Nature Picture Library/Alamy Stock Photo; 17, © Fred Muller/Biosphoto; 17BR, © Thorsten Spoerlein/Adobe Stock; 18, © Thorsten Spoerlein/iStock; 19, © Nature Picture Library/Alamy Stock Photo; 20, © Thorsten Spoerlein/Getty Images; 21T, © Pete Oxford/Minden Pictures/SuperStock; 21M, © Pete Oxford/Minden Pictures/SuperStock; 21B, © Pete Oxford/Minden Pictures/SuperStock; 22T, © Kosong/Adobe Stock; 22B, © jan stopka/Adobe Stock; 23, © Milan/Adobe Stock.

Bearport Publishing Company Product Development Team

Publisher: Jen Jenson; Director of Product Development: Spencer Brinker; Editorial Director: Allison Juda; Editor: Cole Nelson; Editor: Tiana Tran; Production Editor: Naomi Reich; Art Director: Kim Jones; Designer: Kayla Eggert; Designer: Steve Scheluchin; Production Specialist: Owen Hamlin

Statement on Usage of Generative Artificial Intelligence

Bearport Publishing remains committed to publishing high-quality nonfiction books. Therefore, we restrict the use of generative AI to ensure accuracy of all text and visual components pertaining to a book's subject. See BearportPublishing.com for details.

Library of Congress Cataloging-in-Publication Data is available at www.loc.gov or upon request from the publisher.

ISBN: 979-8-89577-045-0 (hardcover)
ISBN: 979-8-89577-469-4 (paperback)
ISBN: 979-8-89577-162-4 (ebook)

For more information, write to Bearport Publishing, 3500 American Blvd W, Suite 150, Bloomington, MN 55431.

Contents

AWESOME
Glass Frogs!

SHHH! It's time to hide. A glass frog sits very still on a leaf. With its arms and legs tucked in close to its see-through body, a hungry snake passes right by. Sneaky and **translucent**, glass frogs are awesome!

A GLASS FROG'S BACK IS SOMETIMES COVERED IN WHITE OR YELLOW SPOTS. IT IS LESS SEE-THROUGH THAN OTHER PARTS OF THE BODY.

Tree Climbers

There are more than 160 **species** of glass frogs living in the forests and mountains of Central and South America, and there may be even more yet to be discovered. All glass frogs have long, webbed toes with special pads that help them cling onto leaves and branches. Their see-through skin helps them blend in with their leafy homes.

> GLASS FROGS CAN CLIMB UP TO 100 FEET (30 M) TO REACH THE TREETOPS.

All in the Name

It is pretty *clear* how glass frogs got their name! These small **amphibians** look like they are made of glass. The skin on the undersides of these frogs can change from somewhat see-through when they are awake to very translucent when they sleep. While snoozing, most of the red blood cells in glass frogs move to their **livers**. This makes their skin so clear.

WHEN AWAKE, A GLASS FROG'S RED BLOOD CELLS MOVE THROUGHOUT ITS BODY, MAKING ITS SKIN MOSTLY *OPAQUE*.

9

Hide and Sleep

ZZZZZ! Because glass frogs are up to three times more see-through while sleeping, they can snooze safely through the day. This **camouflage** helps them hide from hungry **predators**, such as snakes, birds, and lizards. When they wake up at night, these frogs are ready to look for their own food.

SOME GLASS FROGS SLEEP ON THE UNDERSIDE OF LEAVES SO PREDATORS LOOKING FROM ABOVE CANNOT SEE THEM.

Hunting at Night

These **nocturnal** hunters jump through the trees in search of **prey**. Often, they snack on insects and spiders, but some glass frogs will even chow down on smaller frogs. *CHOMP!* They can move their keen eyes in different directions to track down their meals. When something tasty is nearby, the frogs nab their prey using sticky tongues.

UNLIKE MOST FROGS, GLASS FROGS HAVE EYES THAT FACE FORWARD. THIS HELPS THEM FOCUS ON THEIR PREY.

Rain Falls, Frogs Move!

During the dry season, glass frogs hide and hunt in the upper branches of trees. When the rainy season begins, the little creatures are on the move. Glass frogs make their way down to lower branches to get ready to find a mate.

GLASS FROGS LIVE IN TREES THAT ARE NEAR STREAMS OR RIVERS.

Living on a Leaf

A **male** glass frog finds a leaf over a stream to live on during mating season. Then, he calls out to find a **female** partner. *PEEP!* Soon after, the female lays a **clutch** of up to 30 eggs on the male's leaf, using a jellylike glue to hold them in place. Then, she climbs back up into the trees.

SOMETIMES, MALE GLASS FROGS WILL MATE WITH MORE THAN ONE FEMALE DURING A SINGLE SEASON.

A clutch of glass frog eggs

Free Fall

The males of some species of glass frogs protect their eggs by sitting on them. Other kinds of glass frogs leave the eggs on their own. About two weeks later, the eggs hatch into **tadpoles**. These baby frogs then wiggle off their leaf into the water below. *SPLASH!* They live at the bottom of the stream for about a year.

THE SPOTTED PATTERN ON A GLASS FROG LOOKS SIMILAR TO EGGS. THIS HELPS CONFUSE PREDATORS AND KEEPS THEM AWAY FROM REAL GLASS FROG EGGS.

From Tadpole to Frog

Glass frog tadpoles use their muscular tails to swim around the stream. They hide under rocks and eat fallen leaves. As the tadpoles grow, their tails get shorter. After a year, young glass frogs grow legs and climb onto the stream's edge as adults. Finally, these awesome animals head high up in the trees, ready to hunt and hide!

SOME GLASS FROGS CAN LIVE FOR UP TO 14 YEARS.

GLASS FROGS ARE AWESOME!
LET'S LEARN EVEN MORE ABOUT THEM.

Kind of animal: As amphibians, glass frogs breathe through their skin and spend part of their lives in water and part on land.

Other amphibians: There are more than 8,000 species of amphibians. This includes toads, salamanders, and newts.

Size: Most glass frogs grow to be only about 1.3 inches (3.3 cm) long. That's about the length of a paperclip.

GLASS FROGS AROUND THE WORLD

Arctic Ocean

EUROPE
ASIA
NORTH AMERICA
Pacific Ocean
Atlantic Ocean
AFRICA
Indian Ocean
Pacific Ocean
SOUTH AMERICA
AUSTRALIA
Southern Ocean
ANTARCTICA

N
W E
S

WHERE GLASS FROGS LIVE

Glossary

amphibians animals whose life cycles include living both on land and in water

camouflage coloring that makes animals blend in with their surroundings

clutch a group of eggs an amphibian lays at one time

female a glass frog that can lay eggs

liver an organ in the body that cleans the blood

male a glass frog that cannot lay eggs

nocturnal active at night

opaque not see-through

predators animals that hunt and eat other animals

prey an animal that is hunted by another animal for food

species groups that animals are divided into, according to similar characteristics

tadpoles baby glass frogs

translucent partially see-through

Index

Read More

Denega, Danielle. *Amphibians (Learn About: Just Discovered Animals).* New York: Scholastic, 2024.

Murray, Julie. *Glass Frog (Unusual Animals).* Minneapolis: Abdo Kids, 2024.

Learn More Online

1. Go to **FactSurfer.com** or scan the QR code below.
2. Enter "**Glass Frog**" into the search box.
3. Click on the cover of this book to see a list of websites.

About the Author

Janie writes books for kids and lesson plans for teachers. She loves nature hikes and taking her three kids to the zoo!